GRAPHIC BIOGRAPHIES

JOHN F. KENNEDY
American ☆ Visionary

by Nathan Olson
illustrated by Brian Bascle

Consultant:
Robert E. Gilbert, PhD
Professor of Political Science
Northeastern University
Boston, Massachusetts

Capstone
press
Mankato, Minnesota

Graphic Library is published by Capstone Press,
1710 Roe Crest Drive, North Mankato, Minnesota 56003.
www.capstonepub.com

Library of Congress Cataloging-in-Publication Data
Olson, Nathan.
John F. Kennedy : American visionary / by Nathan Olson; illustrated by Brian Bascle.
p. cm.—(Graphic library. Graphic biographies)
Includes bibliographical references and index.
Audience: Grades 4-6.
ISBN: 978-0-7368-6852-5 (hardcover)
ISBN: 978-0-7368-7904-0 (softcover pbk.)
1. Kennedy, John F. (John Fitzgerald), 1917–1963—Juvenile literature. 2. Presidents—United States—Biography—Juvenile literature. 3. Graphic novels. I. Bascle, Brian, ill. II. Title. III. Series.
E842.Z9O47 2007
973.922092—dc22
[B] 2006023333

Summary: In graphic novel format, tells the story of John F. Kennedy, the youngest elected U.S. president who is remembered for his lasting impact on civil rights, foreign policy, and the space program.

Designer
Alison Thiele

Editor
Christine Peterson

Editor's note: Direct quotations from primary sources are indicated by a yellow background.

Direct quotations appear on the following pages:

Page 10, quote attributed to John F. Kennedy; page 14, acceptance speech by John F. Kennedy at the Democratic National Convention on July 15, 1960; page 15, from transcripts of the first Kennedy-Nixon debate on September 26, 1960; page 16, from Kennedy's inaugural address on January 20, 1961; page 19, from Kennedy's speech to Congress on May 25, 1961; page 23, from Kennedy's speech in Berlin on June 26, 1963; as documented at the John F. Kennedy Presidential Library and Museum in Boston, Massachusetts (http://www.jfklibrary.org).

Page 11, quote attributed to Joseph Kennedy Jr., as published in *An Unfinished Life: John F. Kennedy 1917–1963* by Robert Dallek (Boston: Little, Brown, and Co., 2003).

Page 22, from Martin Luther King Jr.'s letter from the Birmingham Jail, April 1963; page 23, from King's "I Have a Dream" speech on August 28, 1963; as recorded by the Martin Luther King Jr. Papers Project at Stanford University (http://www.stanford.edu/group/King/mlkpapers).

Printed in the United States 4540

Table of Contents

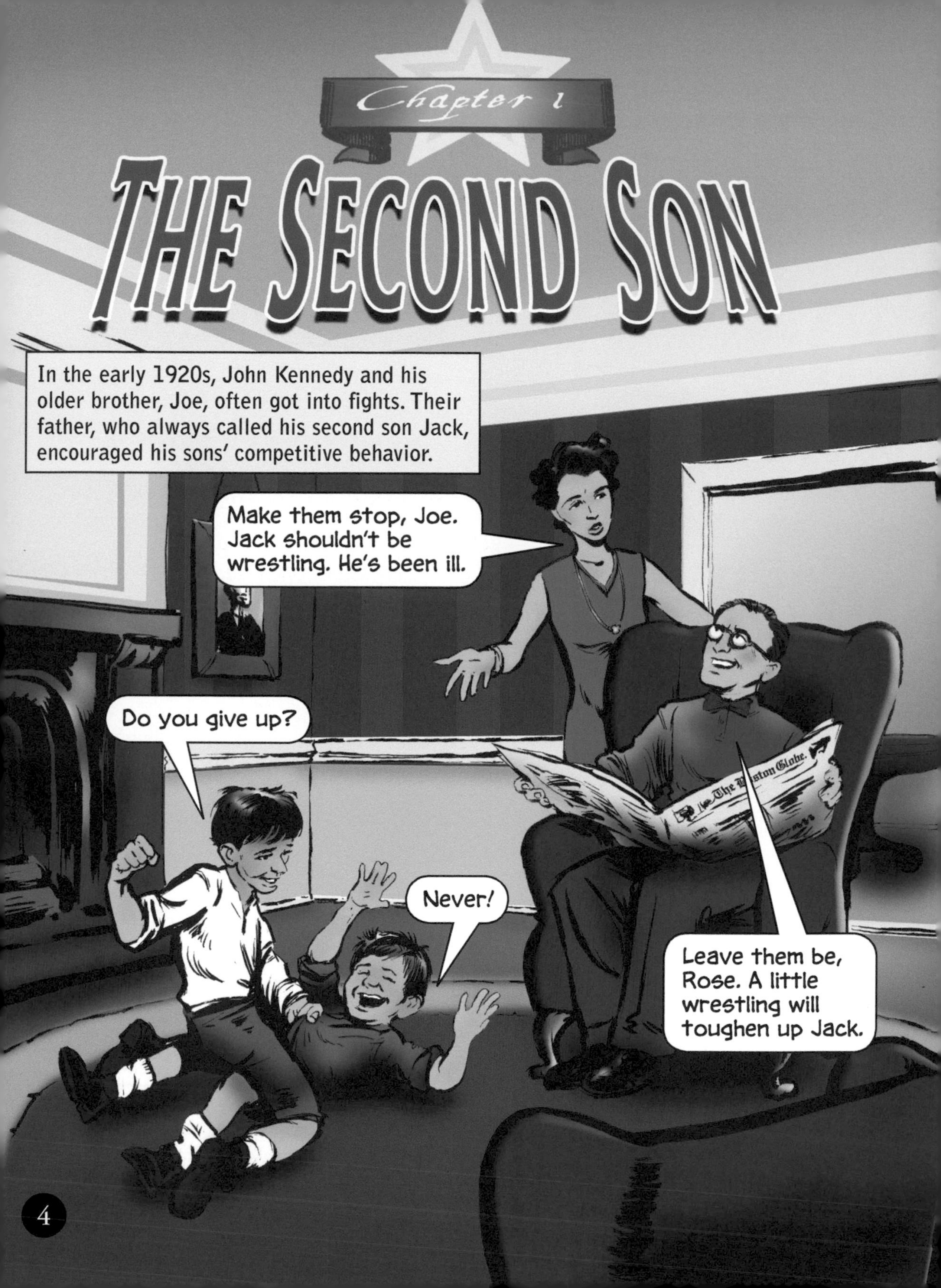
Chapter 1
THE SECOND SON
In the early 1920s, John Kennedy and his older brother, Joe, often got into fights. Their father, who always called his second son Jack, encouraged his sons' competitive behavior.
Make them stop, Joe. Jack shouldn't be wrestling. He's been ill.
Do you give up?
Never!
Leave them be, Rose. A little wrestling will toughen up Jack.
The Boston Globe.

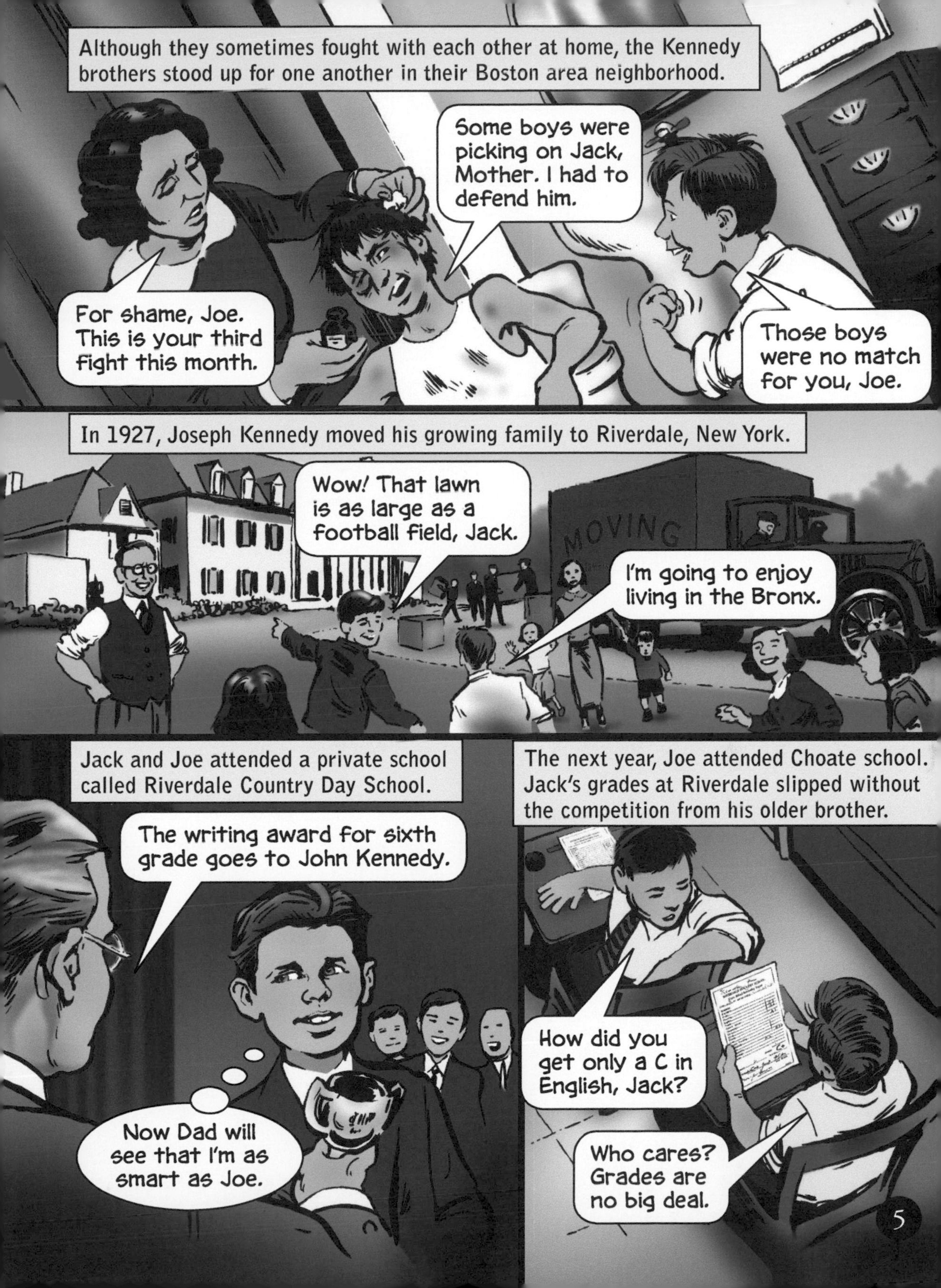
Although they sometimes fought with each other at home, the Kennedy brothers stood up for one another in their Boston area neighborhood.
Some boys were picking on Jack, Mother. I had to defend him.
For shame, Joe. This is your third fight this month.
Those boys were no match for you, Joe.
In 1927, Joseph Kennedy moved his growing family to Riverdale, New York.
Wow! That lawn is as large as a football field, Jack.
MOVING
I'm going to enjoy living in the Bronx.
Jack and Joe attended a private school called Riverdale Country Day School.
The writing award for sixth grade goes to John Kennedy.
Now Dad will see that I'm as smart as Joe.
The next year, Joe attended Choate school. Jack's grades at Riverdale slipped without the competition from his older brother.
How did you get only a C in English, Jack?
Who cares? Grades are no big deal.

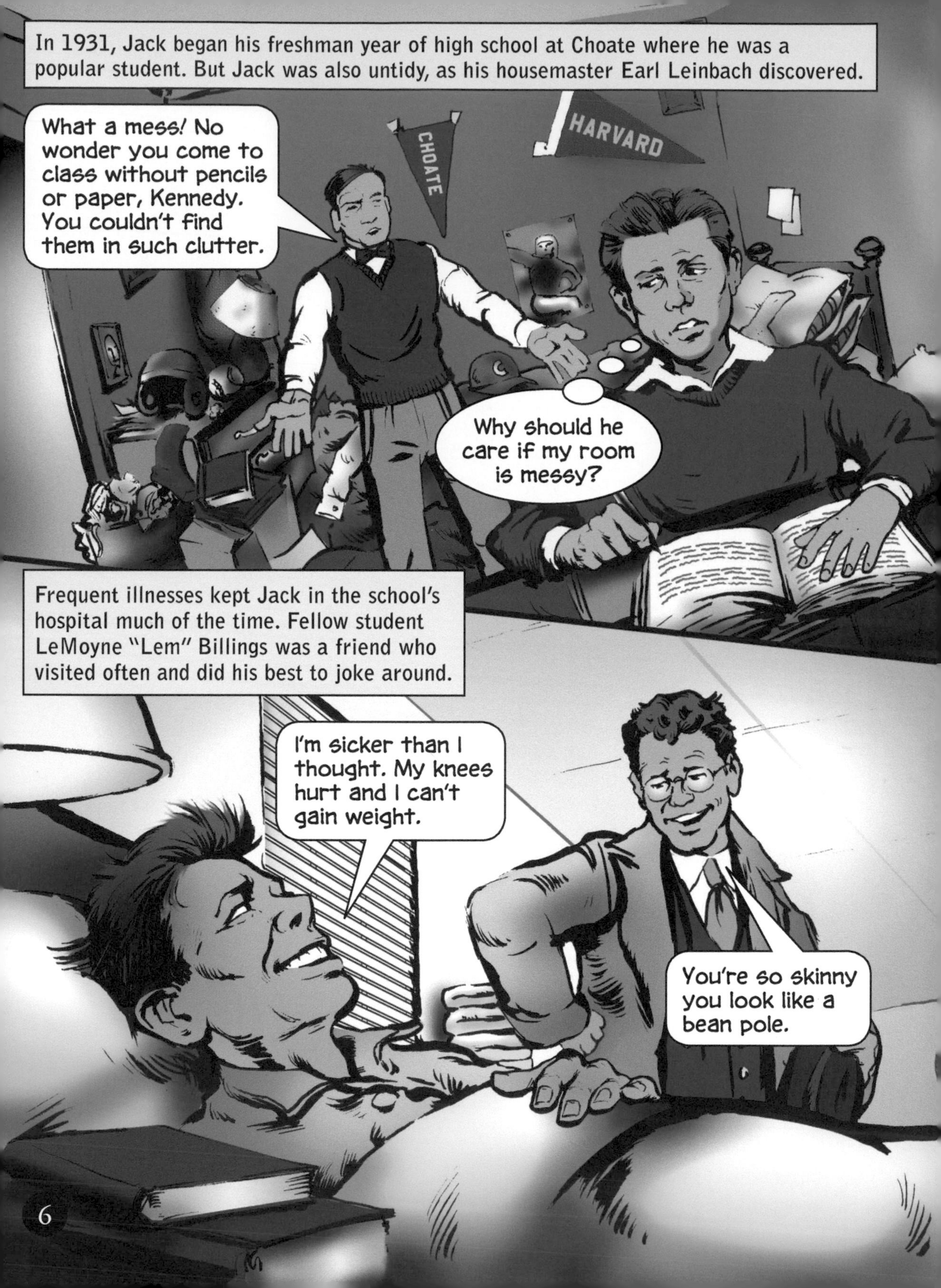
In 1931, Jack began his freshman year of high school at Choate where he was a popular student. But Jack was also untidy, as his housemaster Earl Leinbach discovered.
CHOATE
HARVARD
What a mess! No wonder you come to class without pencils or paper, Kennedy. You couldn't find them in such clutter.
Why should he care if my room is messy?
Frequent illnesses kept Jack in the school's hospital much of the time. Fellow student LeMoyne "Lem" Billings was a friend who visited often and did his best to joke around.
I'm sicker than I thought. My knees hurt and I can't gain weight.
You're so skinny you look like a bean pole.

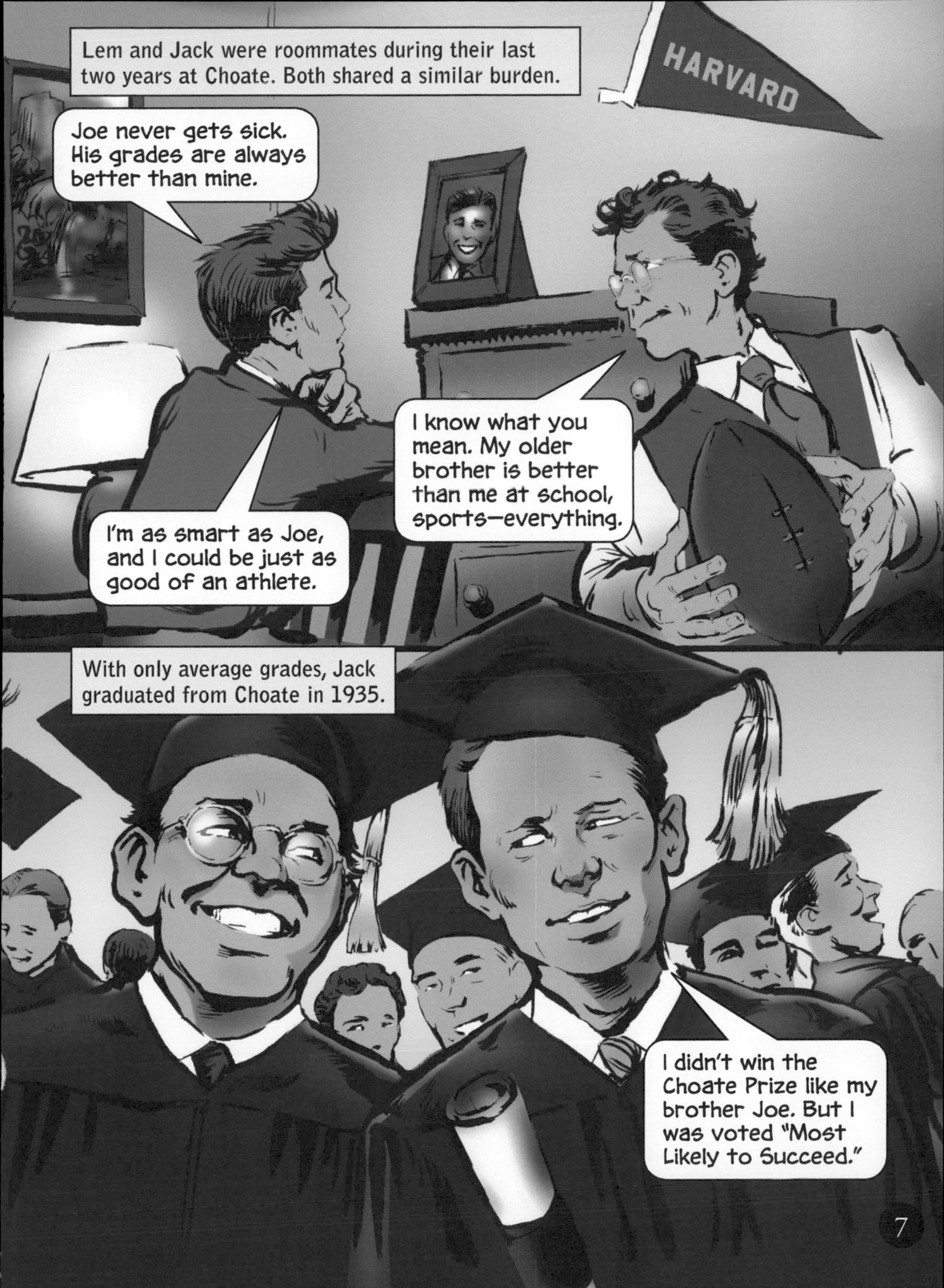
Lem and Jack were roommates during their last two years at Choate. Both shared a similar burden.
HARVARD
Joe never gets sick. His grades are always better than mine.
I know what you mean. My older brother is better than me at school, sports—everything.
I'm as smart as Joe, and I could be just as good of an athlete.
With only average grades, Jack graduated from Choate in 1935.
I didn't win the Choate Prize like my brother Joe. But I was voted "Most Likely to Succeed."

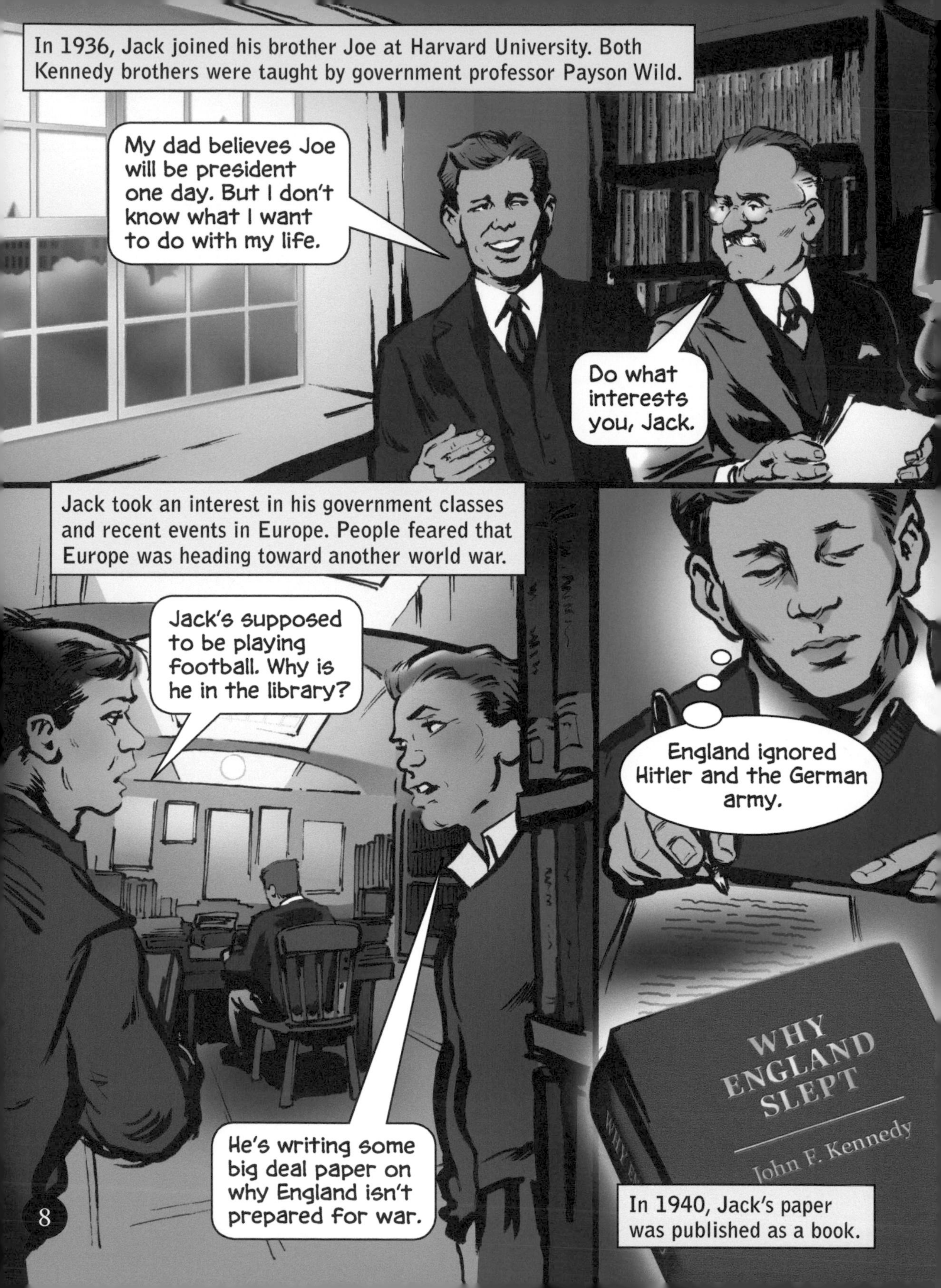
In 1936, Jack joined his brother Joe at Harvard University. Both Kennedy brothers were taught by government professor Payson Wild.
My dad believes Joe will be president one day. But I don't know what I want to do with my life.
Do what interests you, Jack.
Jack took an interest in his government classes and recent events in Europe. People feared that Europe was heading toward another world war.
Jack's supposed to be playing football. Why is he in the library?
He's writing some big deal paper on why England isn't prepared for war.
England ignored Hitler and the German army.
WHY ENGLAND SLEPT
John F. Kennedy
In 1940, Jack's paper was published as a book.

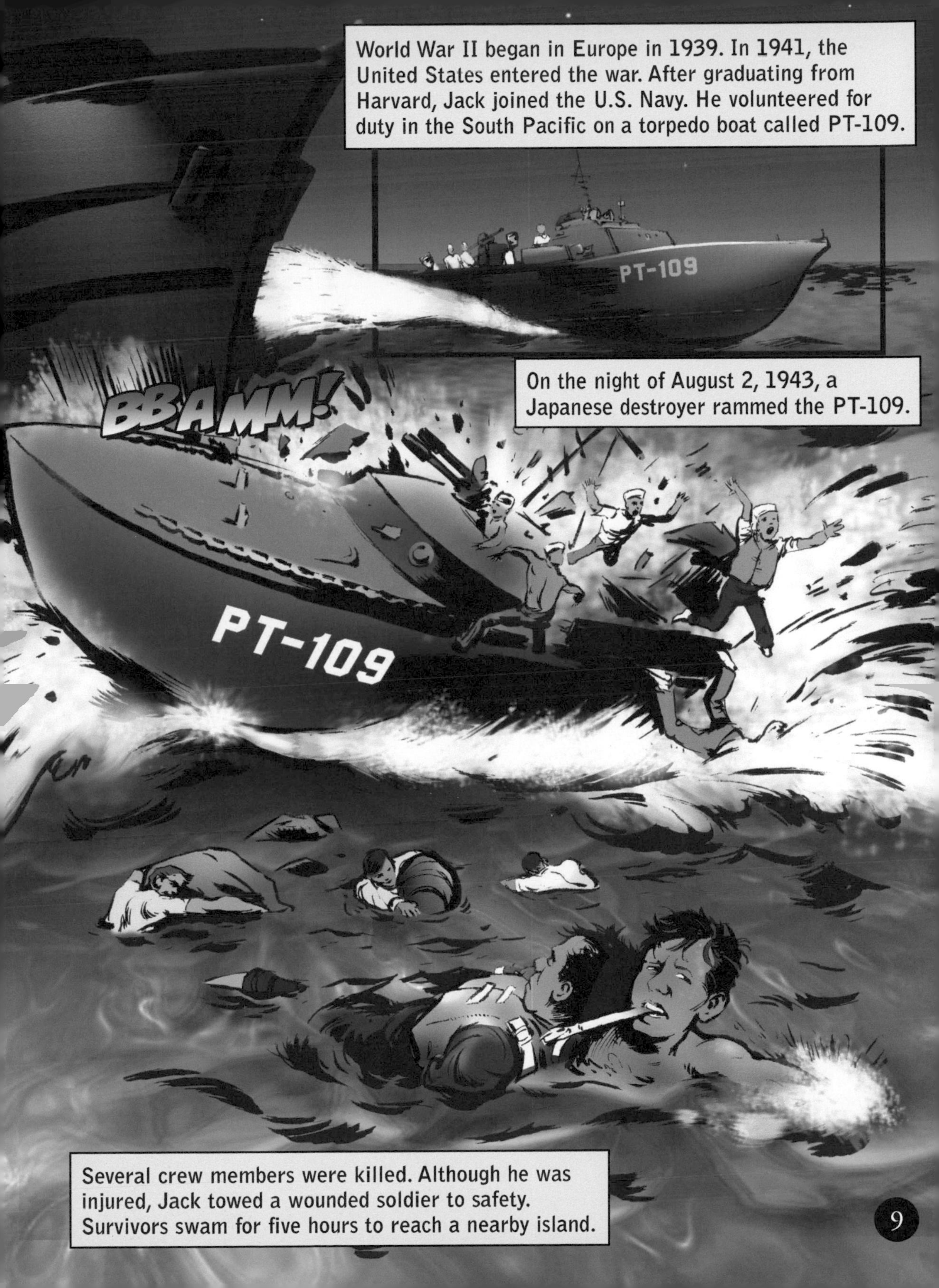

World War II began in Europe in 1939. In 1941, the United States entered the war. After graduating from Harvard, Jack joined the U.S. Navy. He volunteered for duty in the South Pacific on a torpedo boat called PT-109.
PT-109
On the night of August 2, 1943, a Japanese destroyer rammed the PT-109.
BBAMM!
PT-109
Several crew members were killed. Although he was injured, Jack towed a wounded soldier to safety. Survivors swam for five hours to reach a nearby island.

Chapter 2

ROAD TO THE WHITE HOUSE

Back in the United States, people soon learned of Jack's heroic efforts in the Pacific following the PT-109 wreck. Jack was now front-page news.

The Boston Globe

KENNEDY'S SON HERO IN PACIFIC

DOING THEIR SHARE TO SMASH AXIS

PT-109

PT boat rammed by Japanese destroyer; Kennedy rescues crewmember

Hey, Kennedy. I read about you in the paper. How did you become such a hero?

It was easy. They sank my boat.

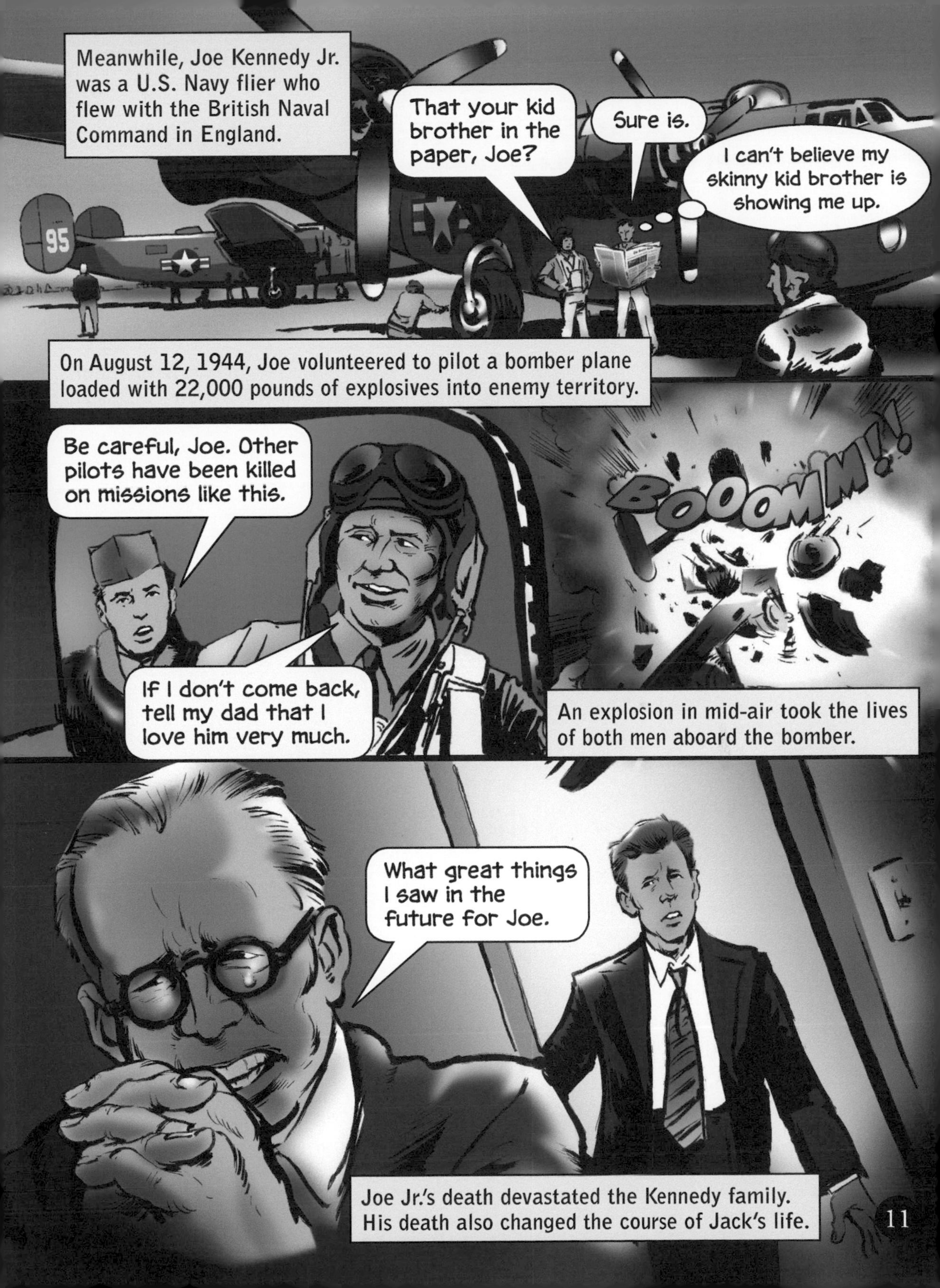
Meanwhile, Joe Kennedy Jr. was a U.S. Navy flier who flew with the British Naval Command in England.
That your kid brother in the paper, Joe?
Sure is.
I can't believe my skinny kid brother is showing me up.
95
On August 12, 1944, Joe volunteered to pilot a bomber plane loaded with 22,000 pounds of explosives into enemy territory.
Be careful, Joe. Other pilots have been killed on missions like this.
If I don't come back, tell my dad that I love him very much.
BOOOMM!!!
An explosion in mid-air took the lives of both men aboard the bomber.
What great things I saw in the future for Joe.
Joe Jr.'s death devastated the Kennedy family. His death also changed the course of Jack's life.

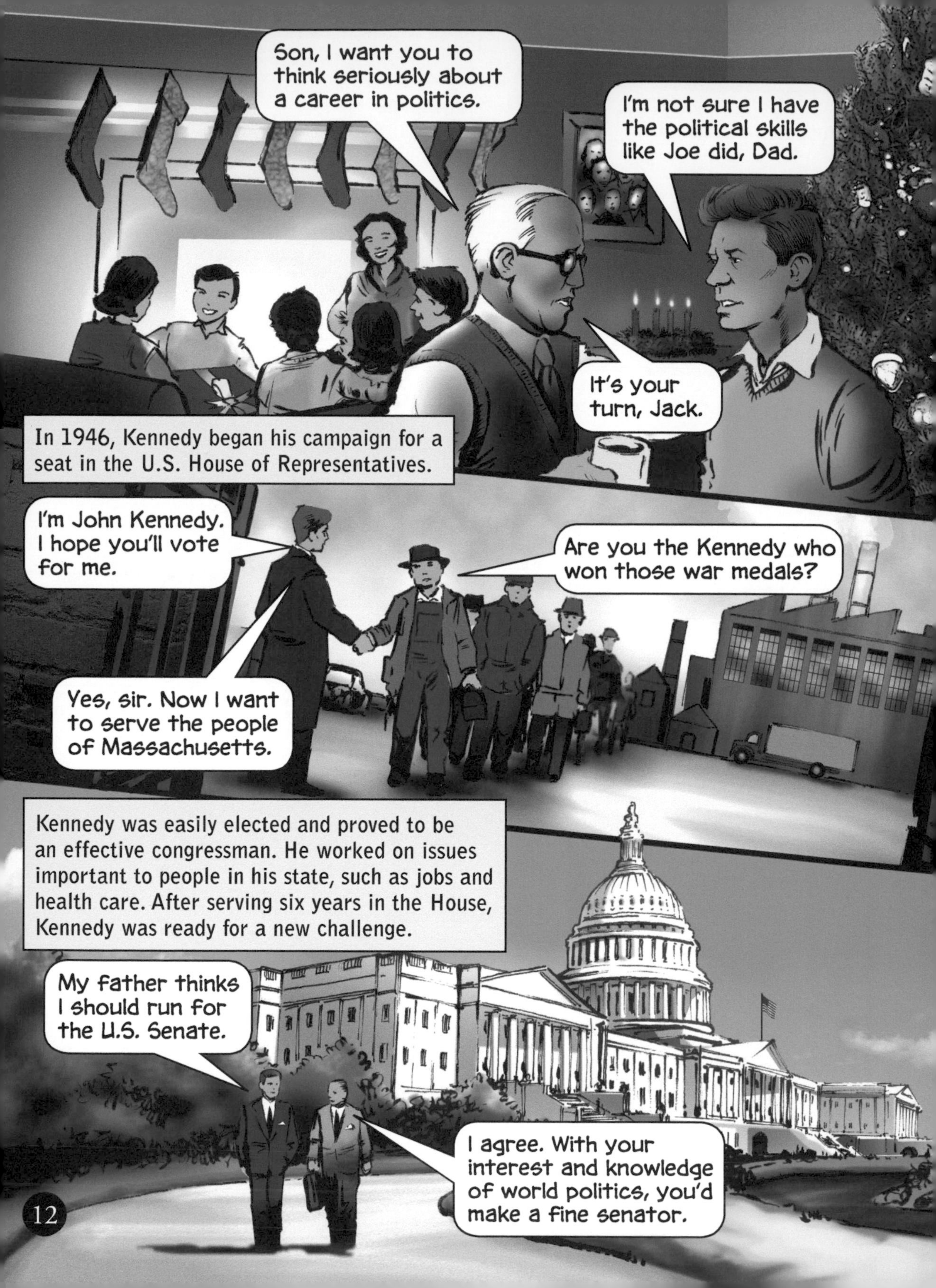
Son, I want you to think seriously about a career in politics.
I'm not sure I have the political skills like Joe did, Dad.
It's your turn, Jack.
In 1946, Kennedy began his campaign for a seat in the U.S. House of Representatives.
I'm John Kennedy. I hope you'll vote for me.
Are you the Kennedy who won those war medals?
Yes, sir. Now I want to serve the people of Massachusetts.
Kennedy was easily elected and proved to be an effective congressman. He worked on issues important to people in his state, such as jobs and health care. After serving six years in the House, Kennedy was ready for a new challenge.
My father thinks I should run for the U.S. Senate.
I agree. With your interest and knowledge of world politics, you'd make a fine senator.

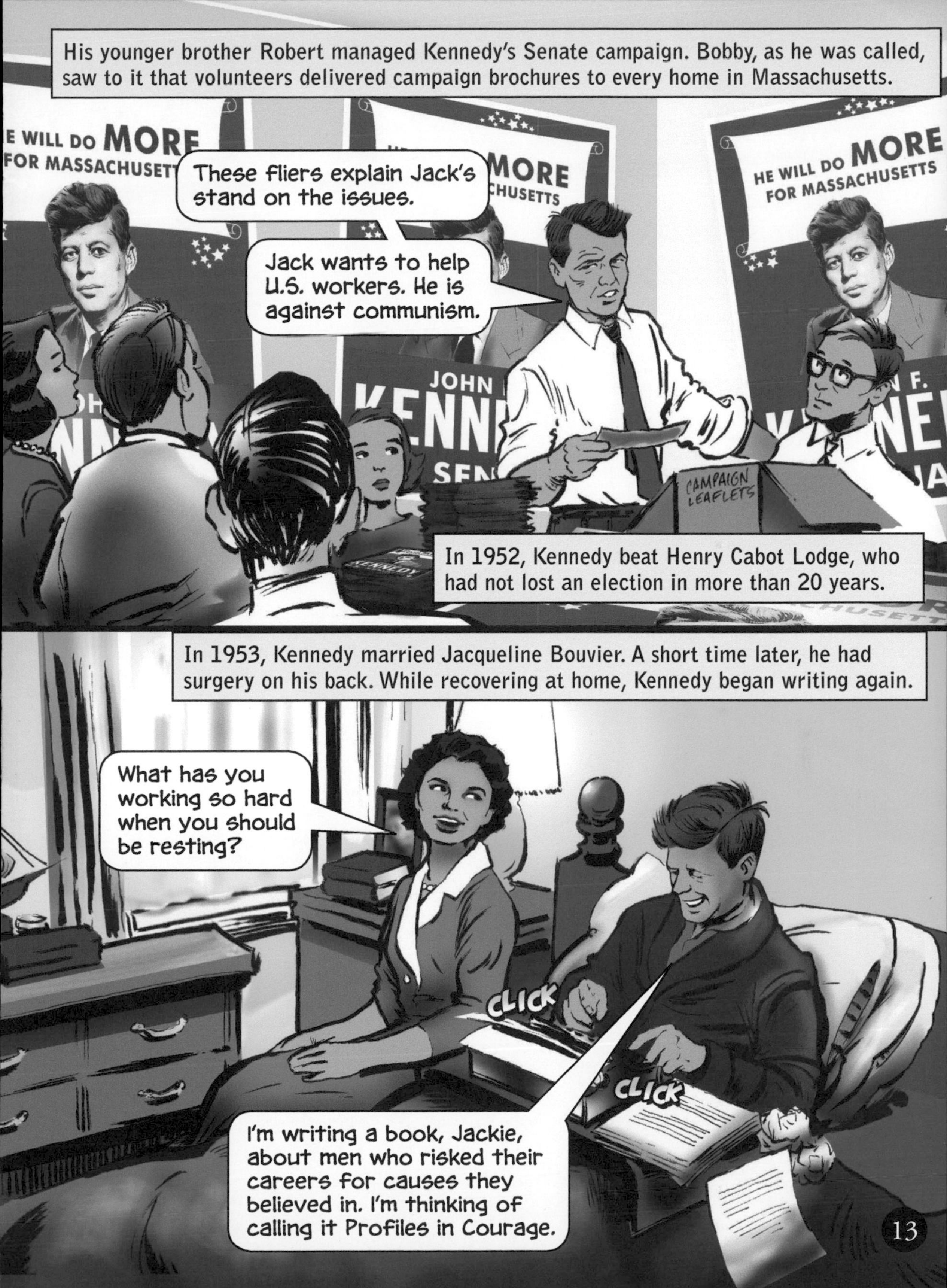
His younger brother Robert managed Kennedy's Senate campaign. Bobby, as he was called, saw to it that volunteers delivered campaign brochures to every home in Massachusetts.
HE WILL DO MORE FOR MASSACHUSETTS
These fliers explain Jack's stand on the issues.
Jack wants to help U.S. workers. He is against communism.
CAMPAIGN LEAFLETS
In 1952, Kennedy beat Henry Cabot Lodge, who had not lost an election in more than 20 years.
In 1953, Kennedy married Jacqueline Bouvier. A short time later, he had surgery on his back. While recovering at home, Kennedy began writing again.
What has you working so hard when you should be resting?
CLICK
CLICK
I'm writing a book, Jackie, about men who risked their careers for causes they believed in. I'm thinking of calling it Profiles in Courage.

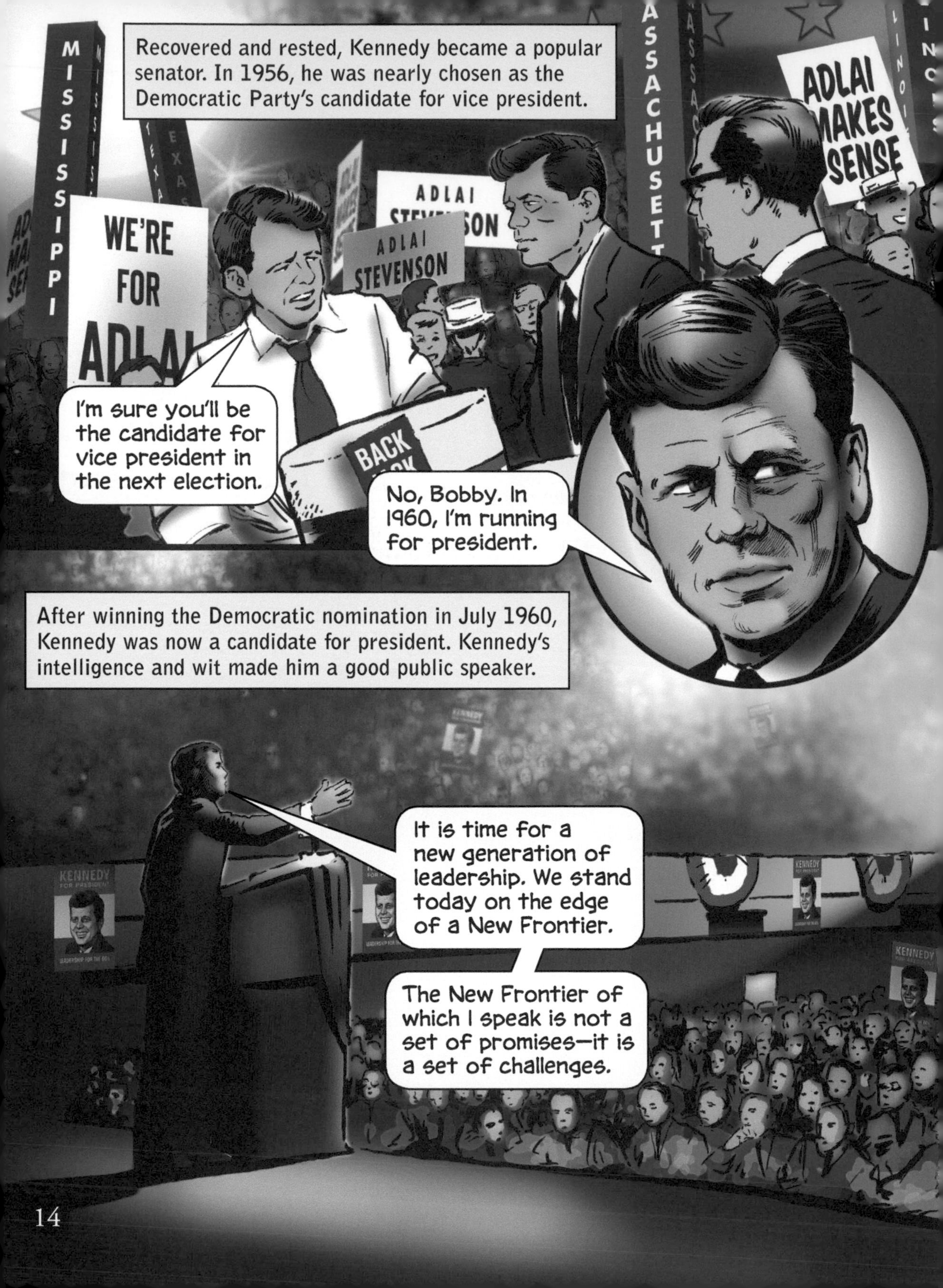
Recovered and rested, Kennedy became a popular senator. In 1956, he was nearly chosen as the Democratic Party's candidate for vice president.
MISSISSIPPI
TEXAS
MASSACHUSETTS
ILLINOIS
WE'RE FOR ADLAI
ADLAI STEVENSON
ADLAI STEVENSON
ADLAI MAKES SENSE
BACK
I'm sure you'll be the candidate for vice president in the next election.
No, Bobby. In 1960, I'm running for president.
After winning the Democratic nomination in July 1960, Kennedy was now a candidate for president. Kennedy's intelligence and wit made him a good public speaker.
KENNEDY FOR PRESIDENT
It is time for a new generation of leadership. We stand today on the edge of a New Frontier.
The New Frontier of which I speak is not a set of promises—it is a set of challenges.

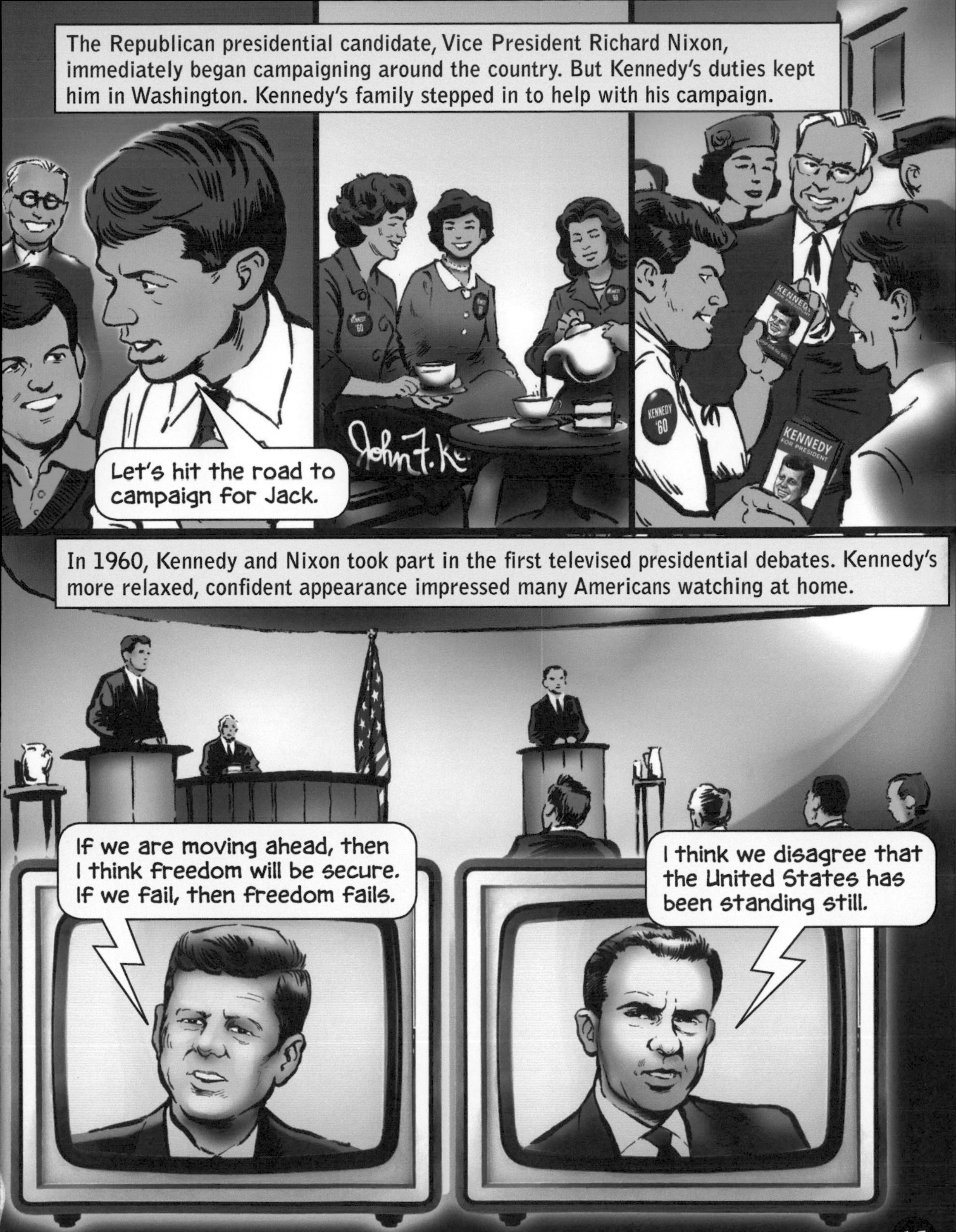

The Republican presidential candidate, Vice President Richard Nixon, immediately began campaigning around the country. But Kennedy's duties kept him in Washington. Kennedy's family stepped in to help with his campaign.
Let's hit the road to campaign for Jack.
KENNEDY '60
KENNEDY FOR PRESIDENT
In 1960, Kennedy and Nixon took part in the first televised presidential debates. Kennedy's more relaxed, confident appearance impressed many Americans watching at home.
If we are moving ahead, then I think freedom will be secure. If we fail, then freedom fails.
I think we disagree that the United States has been standing still.

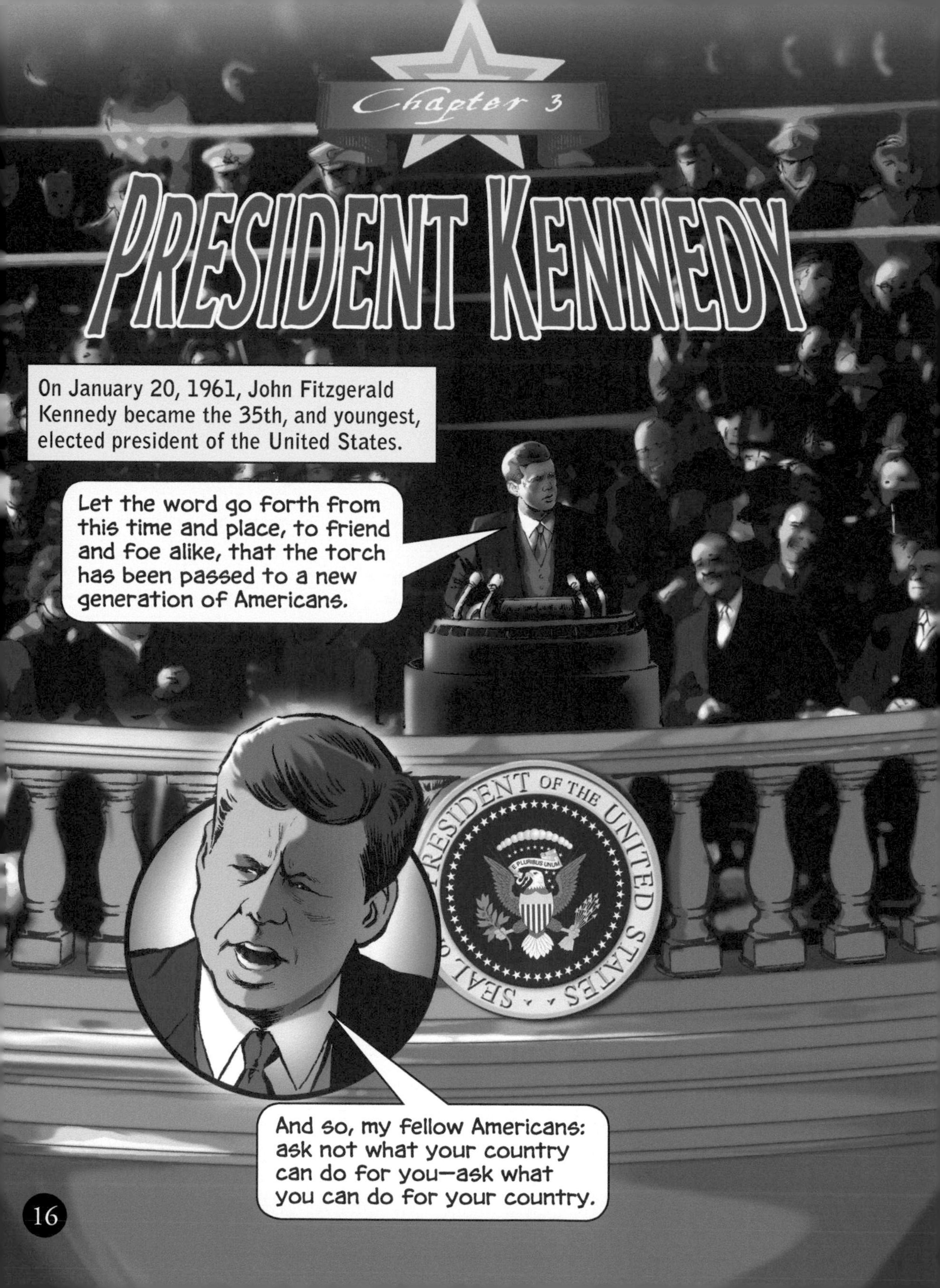
Chapter 3
PRESIDENT KENNEDY
On January 20, 1961, John Fitzgerald Kennedy became the 35th, and youngest, elected president of the United States.
Let the word go forth from this time and place, to friend and foe alike, that the torch has been passed to a new generation of Americans.
SEAL OF THE PRESIDENT OF THE UNITED STATES
E PLURIBUS UNUM
And so, my fellow Americans: ask not what your country can do for you—ask what you can do for your country.

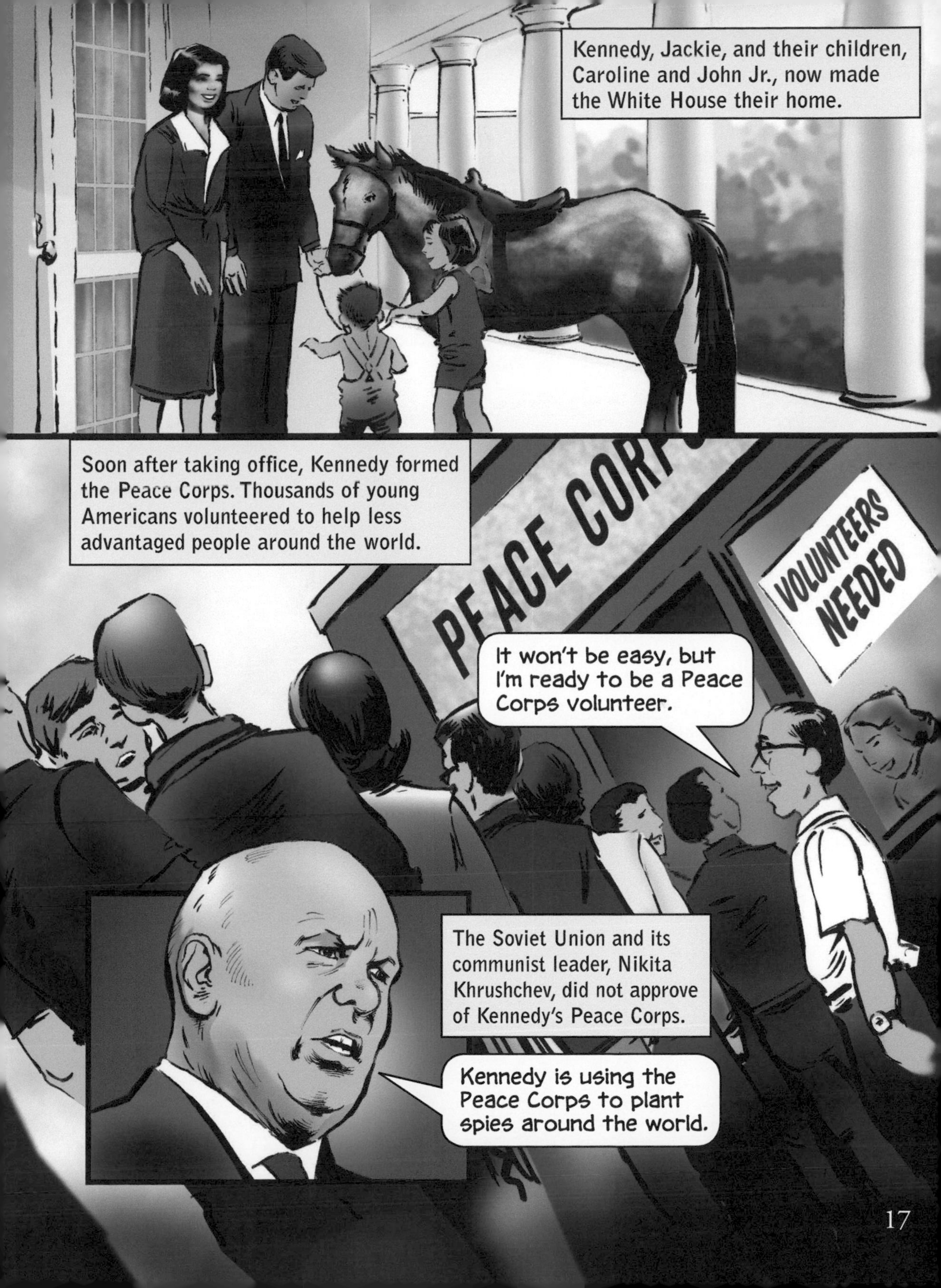
Kennedy, Jackie, and their children, Caroline and John Jr., now made the White House their home.
Soon after taking office, Kennedy formed the Peace Corps. Thousands of young Americans volunteered to help less advantaged people around the world.
PEACE CORP
VOLUNTEERS NEEDED
It won't be easy, but I'm ready to be a Peace Corps volunteer.
The Soviet Union and its communist leader, Nikita Khrushchev, did not approve of Kennedy's Peace Corps.
Kennedy is using the Peace Corps to plant spies around the world.

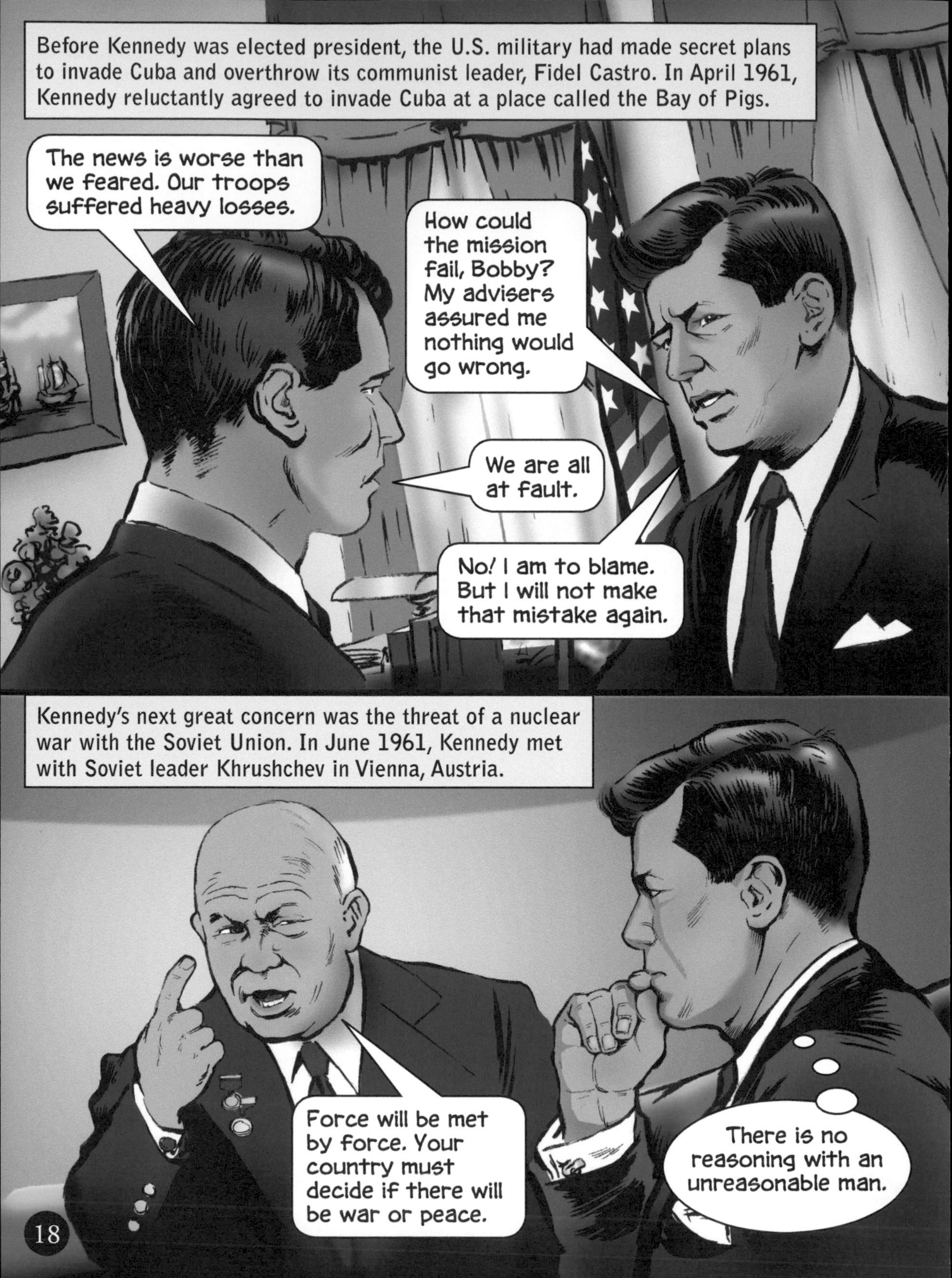
Before Kennedy was elected president, the U.S. military had made secret plans to invade Cuba and overthrow its communist leader, Fidel Castro. In April 1961, Kennedy reluctantly agreed to invade Cuba at a place called the Bay of Pigs.
The news is worse than we feared. Our troops suffered heavy losses.
How could the mission fail, Bobby? My advisers assured me nothing would go wrong.
We are all at fault.
No! I am to blame. But I will not make that mistake again.
Kennedy's next great concern was the threat of a nuclear war with the Soviet Union. In June 1961, Kennedy met with Soviet leader Khrushchev in Vienna, Austria.
Force will be met by force. Your country must decide if there will be war or peace.
There is no reasoning with an unreasonable man.

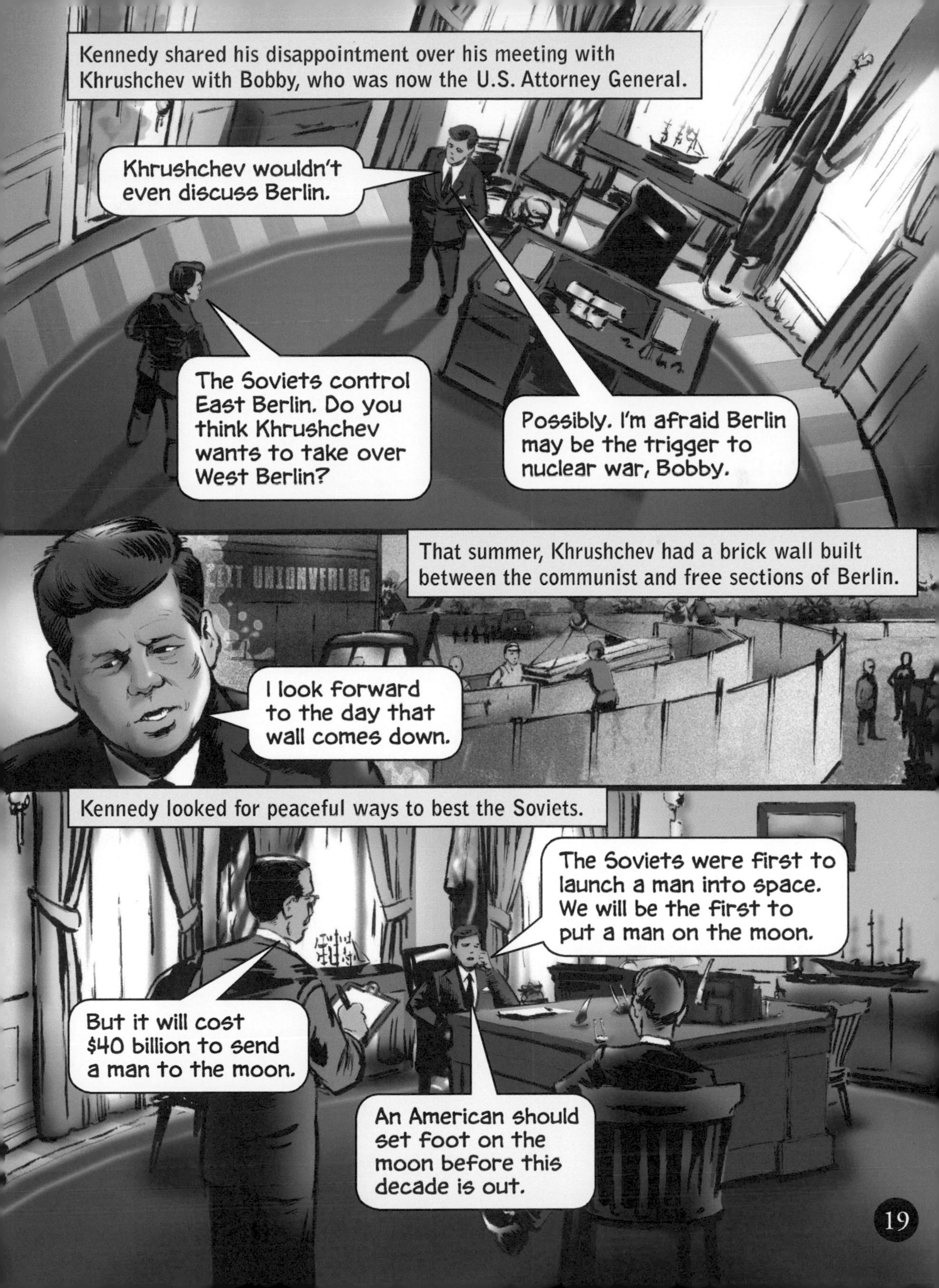
Kennedy shared his disappointment over his meeting with Khrushchev with Bobby, who was now the U.S. Attorney General.
Khrushchev wouldn't even discuss Berlin.
The Soviets control East Berlin. Do you think Khrushchev wants to take over West Berlin?
Possibly. I'm afraid Berlin may be the trigger to nuclear war, Bobby.
That summer, Khrushchev had a brick wall built between the communist and free sections of Berlin.
I look forward to the day that wall comes down.
Kennedy looked for peaceful ways to best the Soviets.
The Soviets were first to launch a man into space. We will be the first to put a man on the moon.
But it will cost $40 billion to send a man to the moon.
An American should set foot on the moon before this decade is out.

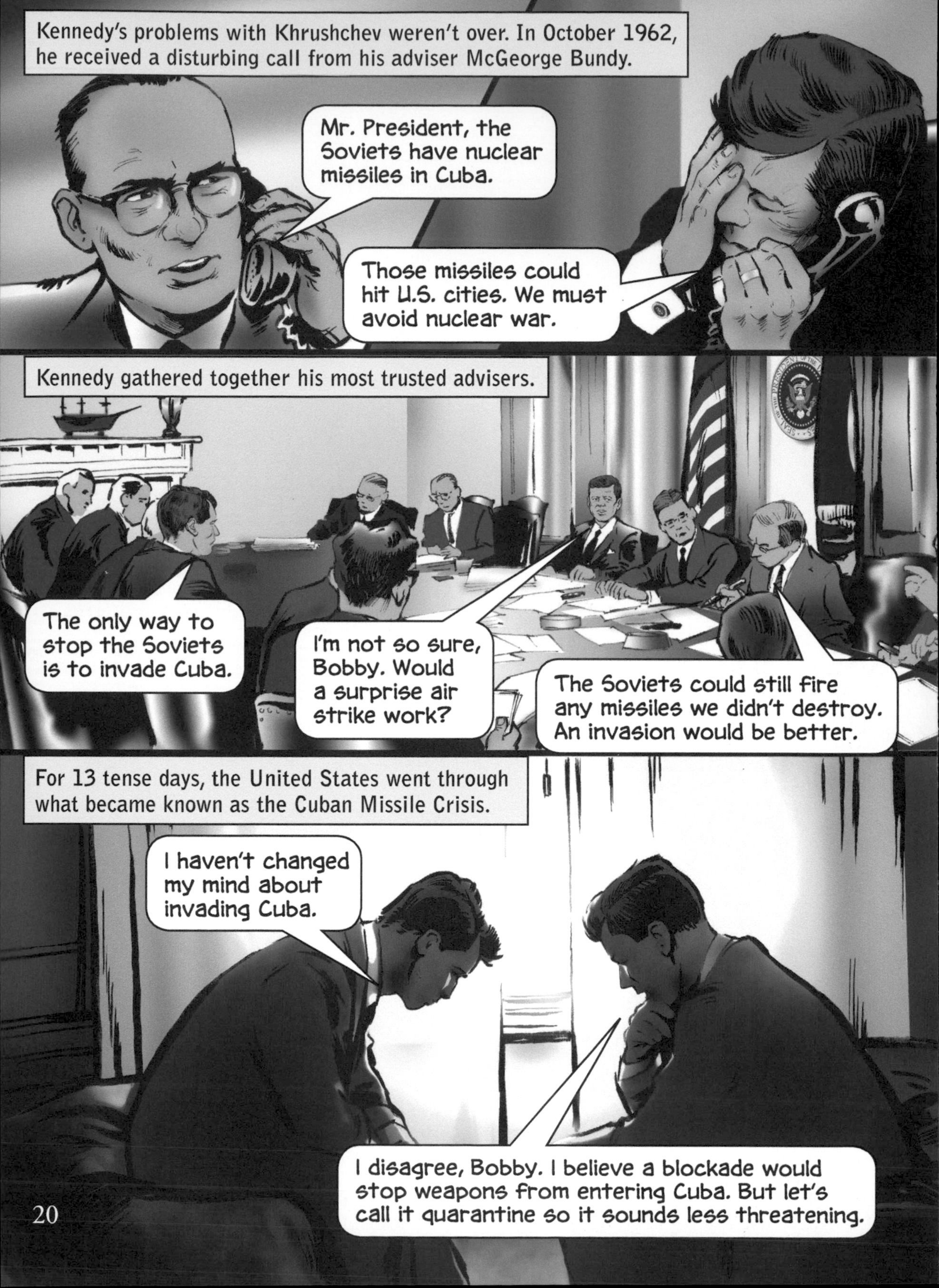
Kennedy's problems with Khrushchev weren't over. In October 1962, he received a disturbing call from his adviser McGeorge Bundy.
Mr. President, the Soviets have nuclear missiles in Cuba.
Those missiles could hit U.S. cities. We must avoid nuclear war.
Kennedy gathered together his most trusted advisers.
The only way to stop the Soviets is to invade Cuba.
I'm not so sure, Bobby. Would a surprise air strike work?
The Soviets could still fire any missiles we didn't destroy. An invasion would be better.
For 13 tense days, the United States went through what became known as the Cuban Missile Crisis.
I haven't changed my mind about invading Cuba.
I disagree, Bobby. I believe a blockade would stop weapons from entering Cuba. But let's call it quarantine so it sounds less threatening.

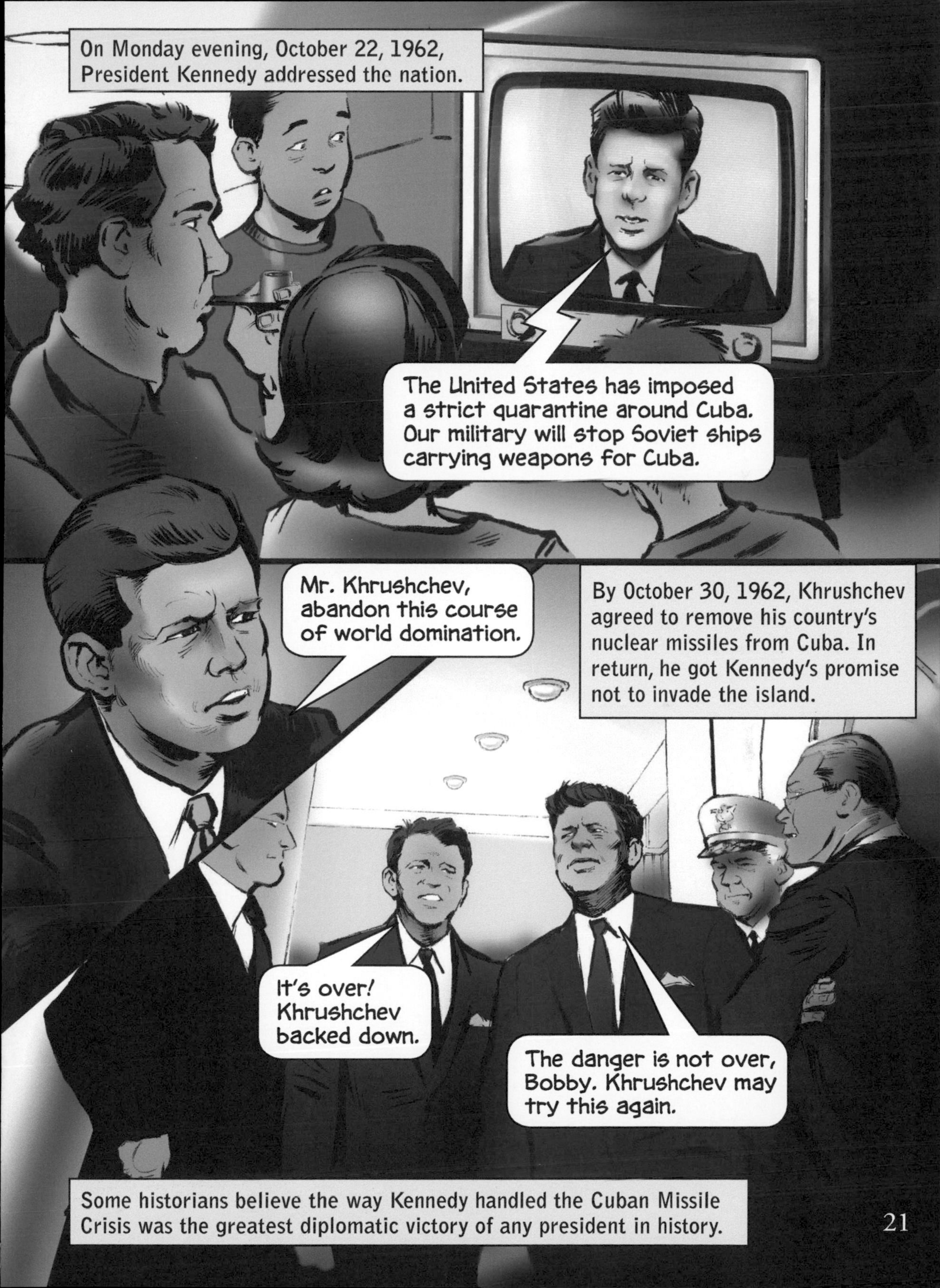
On Monday evening, October 22, 1962, President Kennedy addressed the nation.
The United States has imposed a strict quarantine around Cuba. Our military will stop Soviet ships carrying weapons for Cuba.
Mr. Khrushchev, abandon this course of world domination.
By October 30, 1962, Khrushchev agreed to remove his country's nuclear missiles from Cuba. In return, he got Kennedy's promise not to invade the island.
It's over! Khrushchev backed down.
The danger is not over, Bobby. Khrushchev may try this again.
Some historians believe the way Kennedy handled the Cuban Missile Crisis was the greatest diplomatic victory of any president in history.

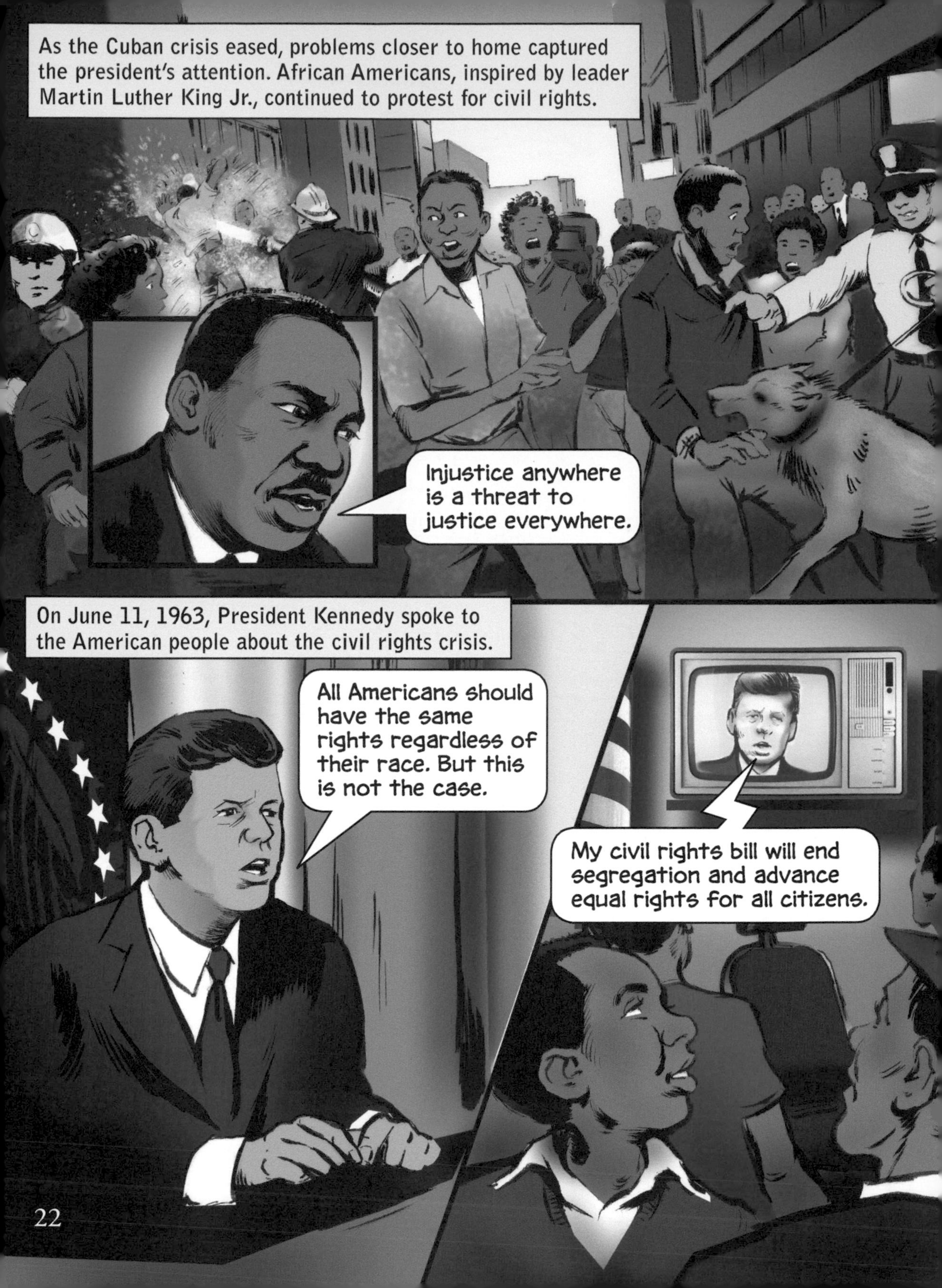
As the Cuban crisis eased, problems closer to home captured the president's attention. African Americans, inspired by leader Martin Luther King Jr., continued to protest for civil rights.
Injustice anywhere is a threat to justice everywhere.
On June 11, 1963, President Kennedy spoke to the American people about the civil rights crisis.
All Americans should have the same rights regardless of their race. But this is not the case.
My civil rights bill will end segregation and advance equal rights for all citizens.

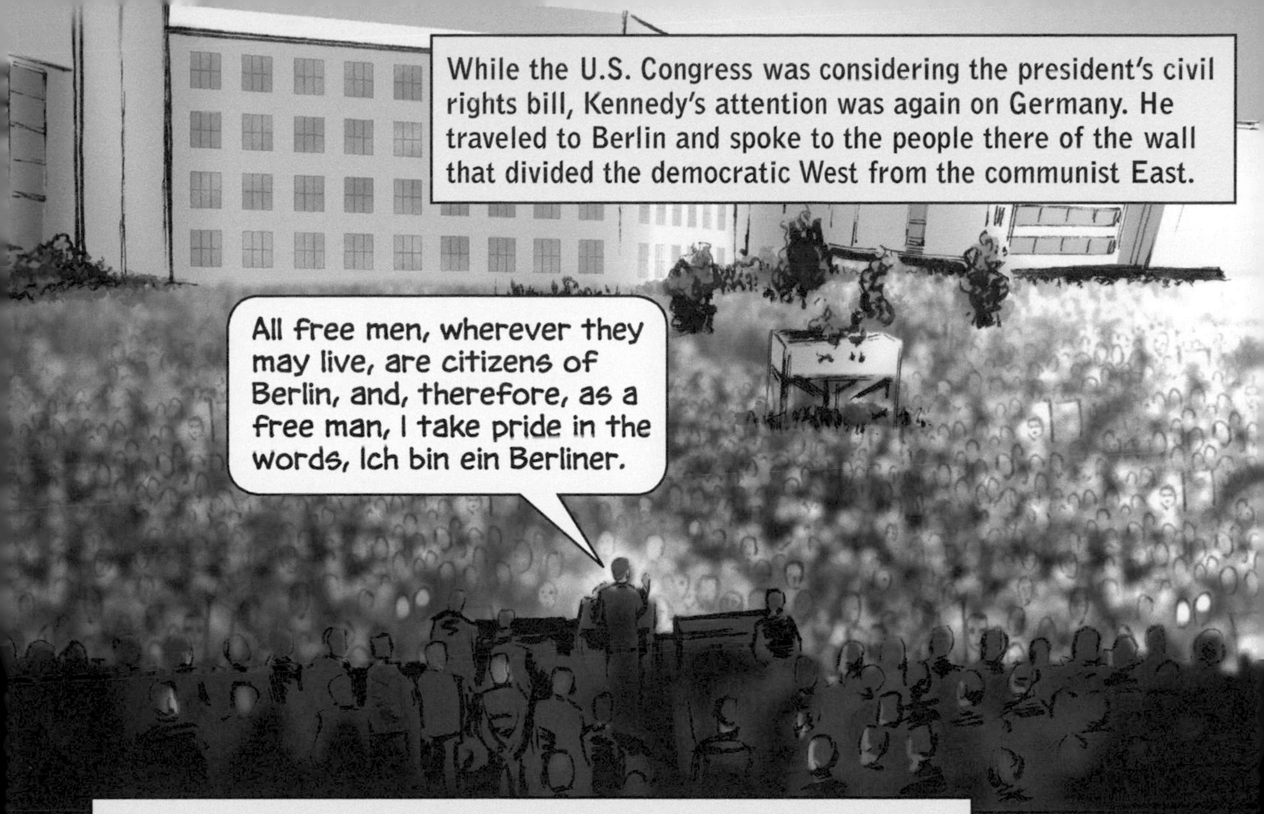
While the U.S. Congress was considering the president's civil rights bill, Kennedy's attention was again on Germany. He traveled to Berlin and spoke to the people there of the wall that divided the democratic West from the communist East.
All free men, wherever they may live, are citizens of Berlin, and, therefore, as a free man, I take pride in the words, Ich bin ein Berliner.

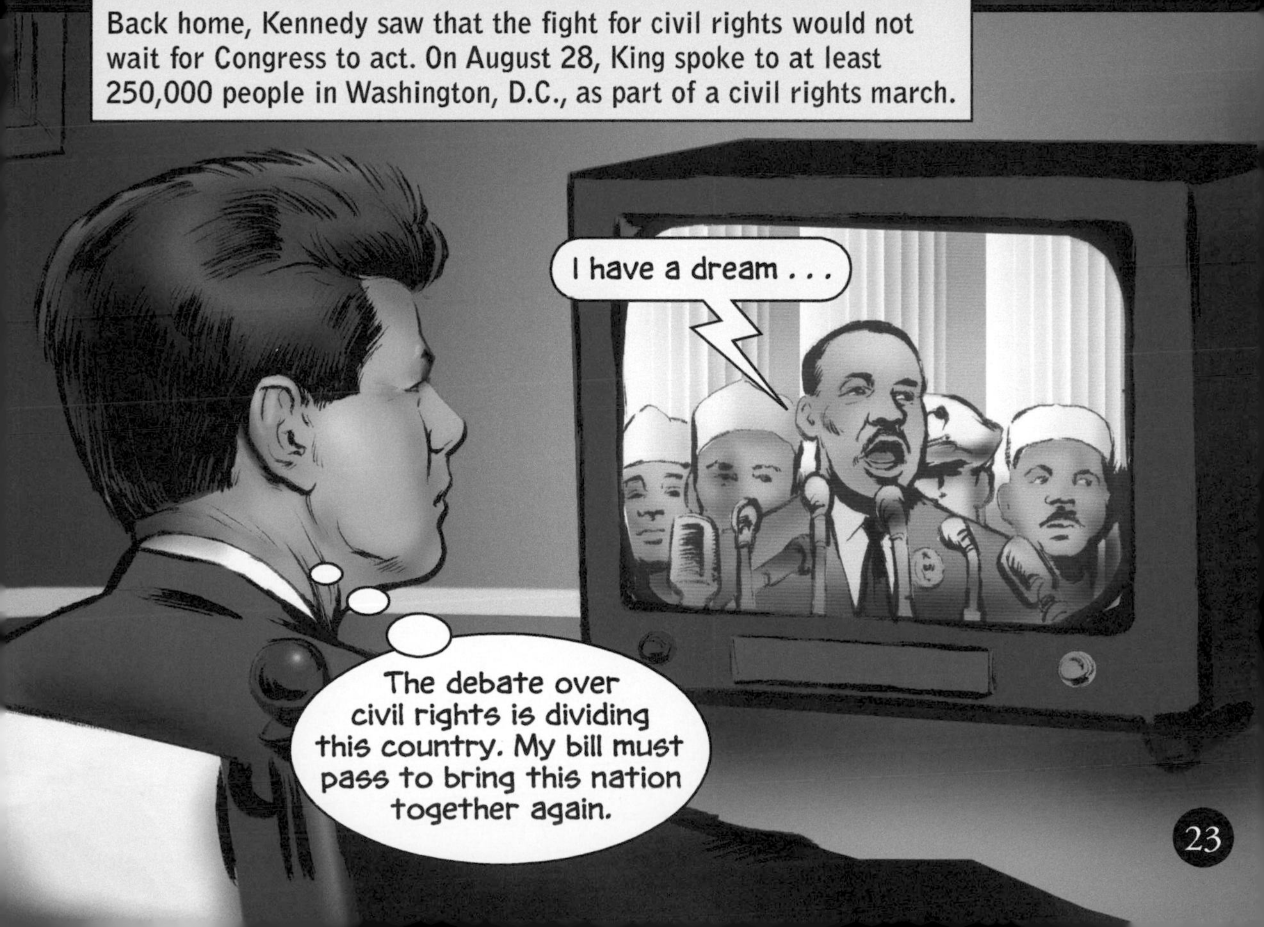
Back home, Kennedy saw that the fight for civil rights would not wait for Congress to act. On August 28, King spoke to at least 250,000 people in Washington, D.C., as part of a civil rights march.
I have a dream . . .
The debate over civil rights is dividing this country. My bill must pass to bring this nation together again.

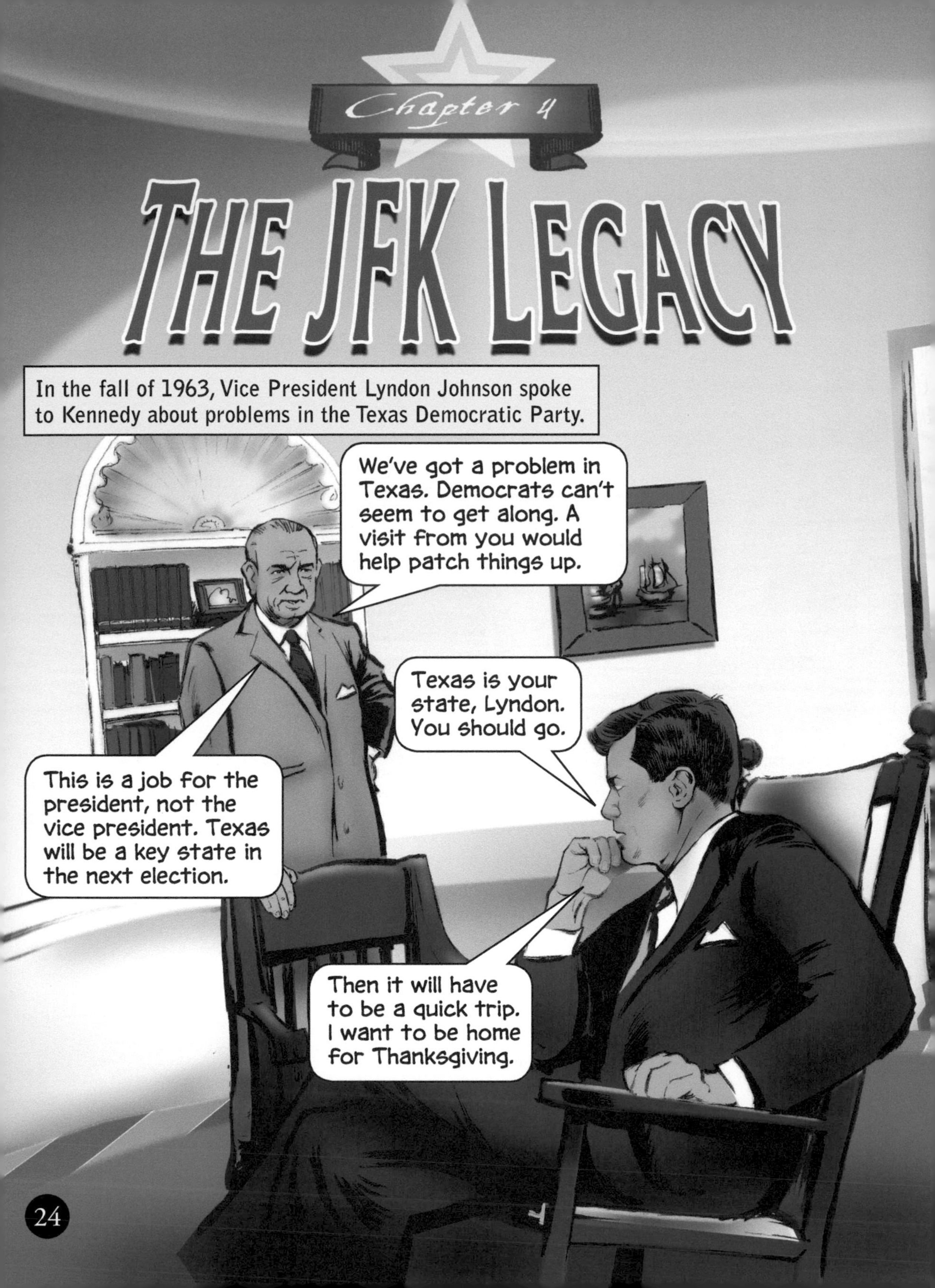
Chapter 4
THE JFK LEGACY
In the fall of 1963, Vice President Lyndon Johnson spoke to Kennedy about problems in the Texas Democratic Party.
We've got a problem in Texas. Democrats can't seem to get along. A visit from you would help patch things up.
Texas is your state, Lyndon. You should go.
This is a job for the president, not the vice president. Texas will be a key state in the next election.
Then it will have to be a quick trip. I want to be home for Thanksgiving.

At 11:40 in the morning on November 22, 1963, President and Mrs. Kennedy arrived to a cheering crowd in Dallas, Texas.

As the Kennedys' motorcade traveled along the parade route in Dallas, three shots rang out. An hour later, President Kennedy was dead.

Kennedy's death shocked the nation. Thousands of people paid their respects to the fallen leader.

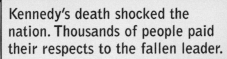

At Kennedy's funeral, his flag-draped coffin made its way through the streets of Washington, D.C. On his son's third birthday, John Fitzgerald Kennedy was laid to rest.

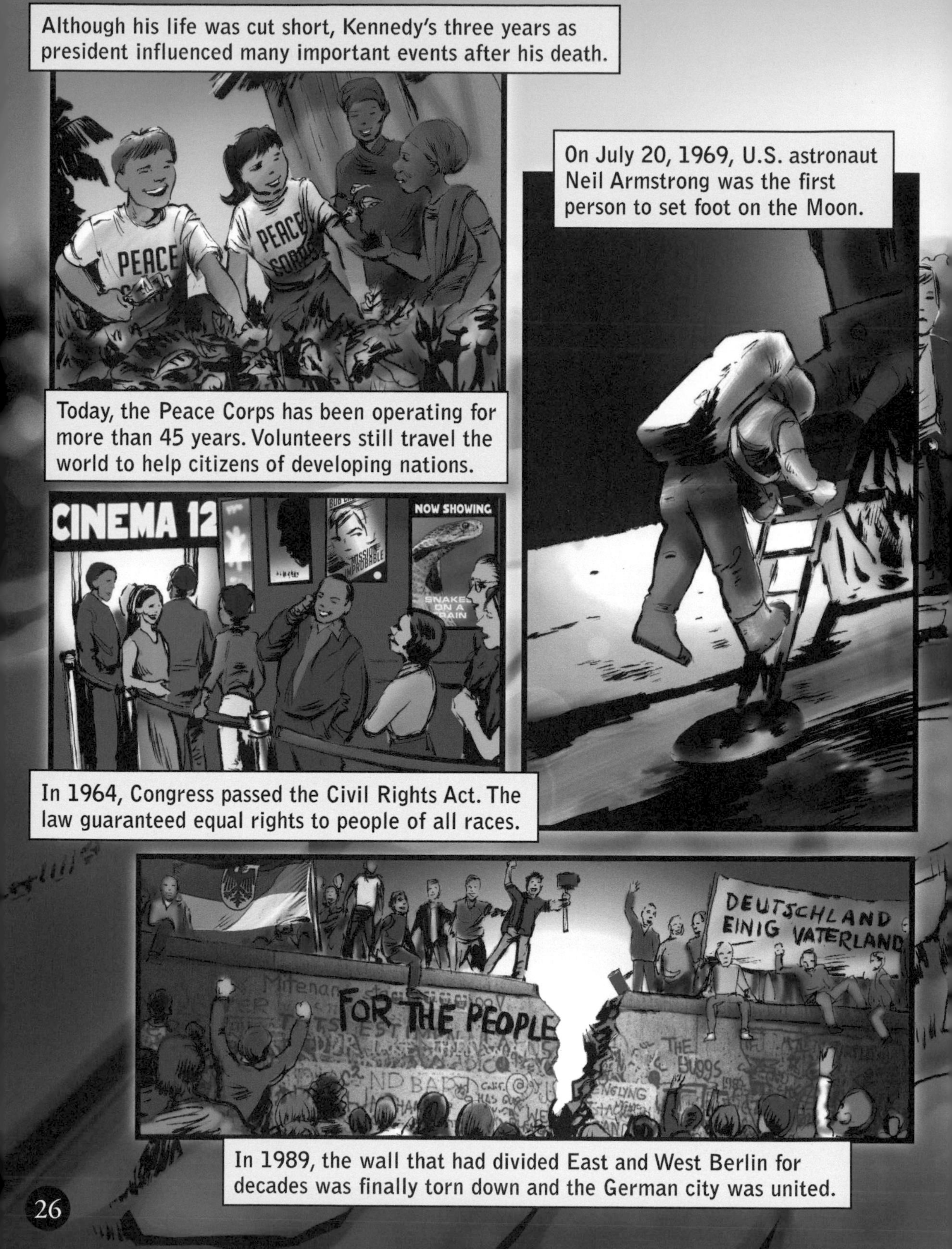
Although his life was cut short, Kennedy's three years as president influenced many important events after his death.
PEACE
PEACE CORPS
Today, the Peace Corps has been operating for more than 45 years. Volunteers still travel the world to help citizens of developing nations.
CINEMA 12
NOW SHOWING
MISSION IMPROBABLE
SNAKES ON A TRAIN
In 1964, Congress passed the Civil Rights Act. The law guaranteed equal rights to people of all races.
On July 20, 1969, U.S. astronaut Neil Armstrong was the first person to set foot on the Moon.
FOR THE PEOPLE
DEUTSCHLAND EINIG VATERLAND
In 1989, the wall that had divided East and West Berlin for decades was finally torn down and the German city was united.

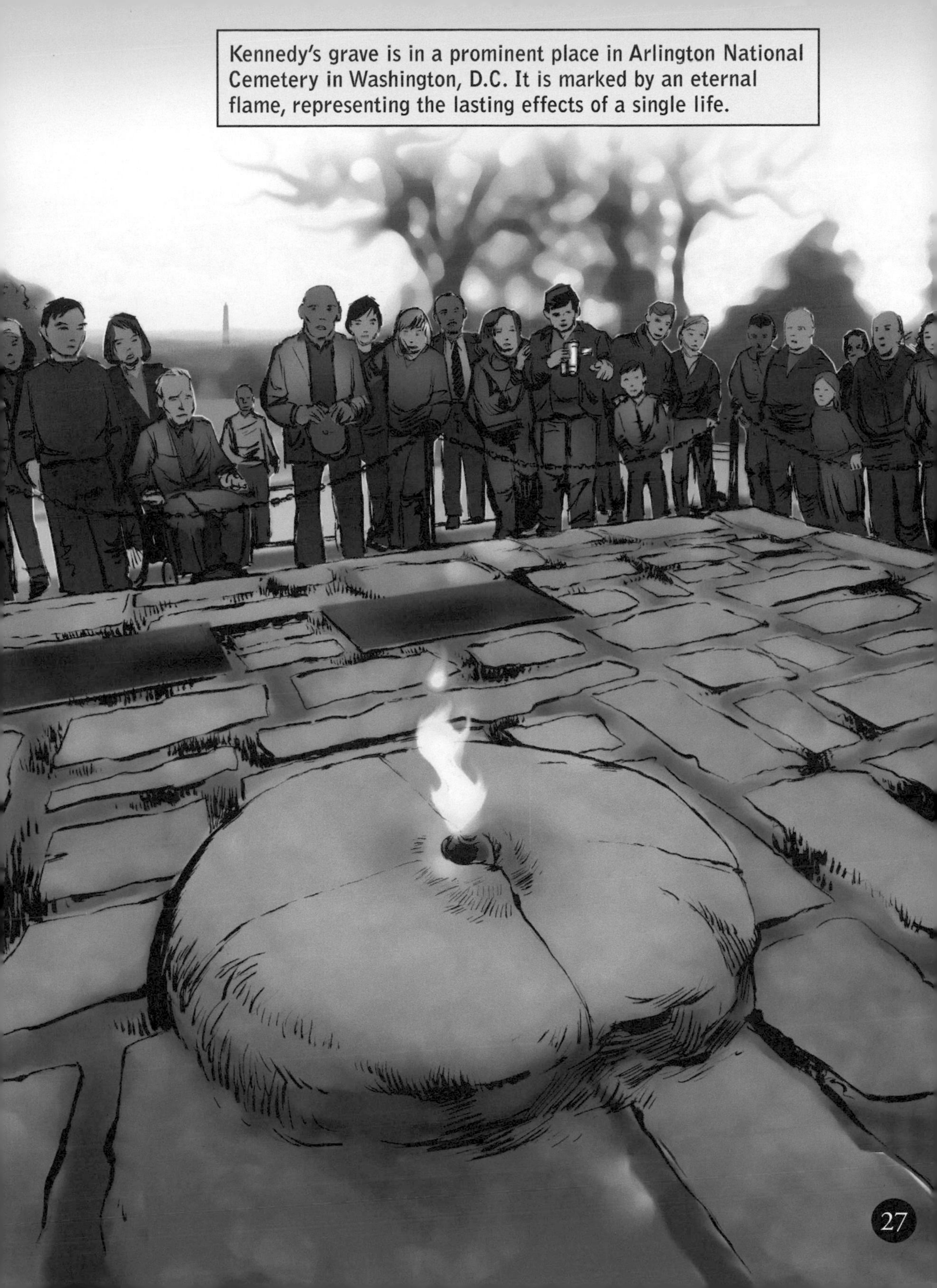
Kennedy's grave is in a prominent place in Arlington National Cemetery in Washington, D.C. It is marked by an eternal flame, representing the lasting effects of a single life.

JOHN F. KENNEDY

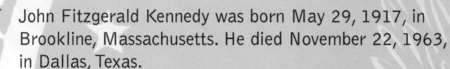

☆ John Fitzgerald Kennedy was born May 29, 1917, in Brookline, Massachusetts. He died November 22, 1963, in Dallas, Texas.

☆ Kennedy was the youngest man ever to be elected U.S. president. He was also the youngest president to die while in office.

☆ Kennedy's middle name, Fitzgerald, was in honor of his mother's father, John Francis Fitzgerald. Once Kennedy was elected president, newspapers began referring to him as JFK. His initials took up less space in headlines than his name.

☆ When Kennedy was a student at Choate, he was briefly expelled for one of his many pranks. He was able to return to school and graduated 65th out of a class of 110 students. His friends named him "Most Likely to Succeed."

☆ Kennedy and his wife, Jackie, had their first child, Caroline, on November 27, 1957. Their second child, John Jr., was born November 25, 1960. The couple's second son and third child, Patrick, was born August 7, 1963. He died two days later.

After the first Kennedy-Nixon debate, people had different opinions on who won the debate. People who listened to the debate on the radio believed Nixon had done a better job. But people who watched the event on TV thought Kennedy won the debate.

 Throughout his life, Kennedy had a number of medical problems including severe back pain and Addison's disease, which affects the body's adrenal glands. Kennedy wore a back brace throughout his presidency. He found that sitting in a rocking chair was most comfortable.

 Who fired the bullet that killed President Kennedy? Dallas police arrested Lee Harvey Oswald for the president's murder. Oswald was shot and killed by Jack Ruby while in police custody. Many people, however, believed that several gunmen were involved in a plan to kill Kennedy. Officially, Oswald is considered to be the only gunman, shooting from a sixth floor window of the Texas School Book Depository. Today, the sixth floor of this building is a museum devoted to the events of November 22, 1963.

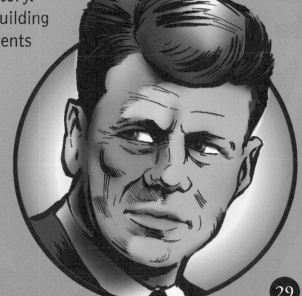

GLOSSARY

assure (uh-SHUR)—to promise something

blockade (blok-ADE)—a closing off of an area to keep people or supplies from going in or out

communism (KOM-yuh-niz-uhm)—a way of organizing a country so that all the land, houses, and factories belong to the government, and the profits are shared by all

crisis (KRYE-siss)—a time of danger and difficulty

diplomatic (dip-luh-MAT-ik)—being good at dealing with people

quarantine (KWOR-uhn-teen)—the act of keeping others away from a certain area

Soviet Union (SOH-vee-et YOON-yuhn)—a former federation of 15 republics that included Russia, Ukraine, and other nations of eastern Europe and northern Asia; also called the Union of Soviet Socialist Republics (USSR).

INTERNET SITES

FactHound offers a safe, fun way to find Internet sites related to this book. All of the sites on FactHound have been researched by our staff.

Here's how:
1. Visit *www.facthound.com*
2. Choose your grade level.
3. Type in this book ID **0736868526** for age-appropriate sites. You may also browse subjects by clicking on letters, or by clicking on pictures and words.
4. Click on the **Fetch It** button.

FactHound will fetch the best sites for you!

READ MORE

Ashby, Ruth. *John and Jacqueline Kennedy.* Presidents and First Ladies. Milwaukee: World Almanac Library, 2005.

Byrne, Paul J. *The Cuban Missile Crisis: To the Brink of War.* Snapshots in History. Minneapolis: Compass Point Books, 2006.

Kaplan, Howard S. *John F. Kennedy.* DK Biography. New York: DK Publishing, 2004.

Supples, Kevin. *The Civil Rights Movement.* People Who Changed America. Washington, D.C.: National Geographic Society, 2003.

BIBLIOGRAPHY

Dallek, Robert. *An Unfinished Life: John F. Kennedy 1917–1963.* Boston: Little, Brown, and Co., 2003.

Gilbert, Robert E. *The Mortal Presidency: Illness and Anguish in the White House.* New York: Fordham University Press, 1998.

Kennedy, John F. *Profiles in Courage.* New York: Harper, 1956.

O'Brien, Michael. *John F. Kennedy: A Biography.* New York: Thomas Dunne Books/St. Martin's Press, 2005.

INDEX